ALL STAR ENGLISH

AN INTEGRATED ESL CURRICULUM

Patricia Richard-Amato ★ **Charles Skidmore** ★ **Anne Marie Drayton**

Addison-Wesley Publishing Company

ISBN 0-201-88086-5 Softbound
ISBN 0-201-88543-3 Hardbound
1 2 3 4 5 6 7 8 9 10 -WC- 00 99 98 97 96

CONTENTS

LOOK AT ME

Reading Corner

Try these terrific books!

New Kids in Town
by Janet Bode
Immigrant kids tell their stories.

Hello, My Name is Scrambled Eggs
by Jamie Gilson
A Vietnamese boy comes to America.

Friends 4–Ever
by Deirdre Corey
Books about four girls and their friendship.

Hi, My Name is Carmen

Hi, my name is Carmen Ortiz. I'm from Puerto Rico, but I live in New York now. I live with my parents and my brother, José. I am 13 years old. José is 15 years old. We both have brown hair and brown eyes like our parents.

My father is a truck driver. In his spare time, he likes to make things out of wood. He has a workshop in the basement. My mother is an artist. She paints beautiful pictures. People buy her paintings.

New York

USA

Puerto Rico

Art Math Music
Science Social Studies

LANGUAGE ARTS

My favorite color is red, and my favorite thing to wear is my red sweater. I love to read. I go to the library every week because I want to know everything about the world. I want to go to college. I want to be a math teacher or an astronaut.

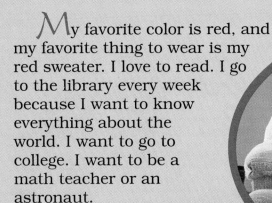

USA

Mexico City

My best friend is Carolina Hernandez. She is from Mexico. We like to go to the mall on weekends. We like to windowshop, but sometimes we buy things.

Carolina loves music. She buys CDs with her allowance. She wants to be a musician. I'm saving my money for college, but sometimes I buy earrings.

Some days, I really miss Puerto Rico. I miss my friends. I miss the food, the music, and the dancing. Other days, I am happy to be in New York. My family is here. My new friends are here. Carolina says, "Carmen, you are my best friend." And then she smiles. I smile, too.

YOUR **T**URN Talk about yourself. Tell a partner about your family. What are your favorite things? What do you like about the United States?

EVERYBODY SAYS

DOROTHY ALDIS

Everybody says
I look just like my mother.
Everybody says
I'm the image of Aunt Bee.
Everybody says
My nose is like my father's
But I want to look like ME!

 YOUR TURN Do you look like anyone in your family? Talk about this with a partner.

Look at Me

Look at the pictures. Answer the questions.

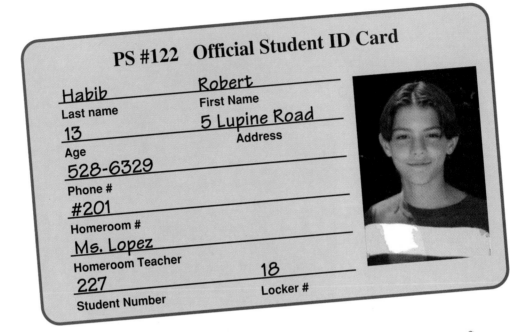

PS #122   Official Student ID Card

Habib — Last name

Robert — First Name

5 Lupine Road — Address

13 — Age

528-6329 — Phone #

#201 — Homeroom #

Ms. Lopez — Homeroom Teacher

227 — Student Number

18 — Locker #

1. What is his first name?
2. What is his last name?
3. How old is he?
4. What is his address?
5. What is his phone number?
6. What is his homeroom number?
7. What is the name of his homeroom teacher?
8. What is his locker number?

Art Math Music
Science Social Studies
LANGUAGE ARTS

1. What is her first name?
2. What is her last name?
3. How old is she?
4. What is her address?
5. What is her phone number?
6. What is her homeroom number?
7. What is the name of her homeroom teacher?
8. What is her locker number?

PS #122   Official Student ID Card

Sanders
Last name

Lucy
First Name

14
Age

25 C Street
Address

528-9248
Phone #

#214
Homeroom #

Mr. Wang
Homeroom Teacher

416
Student Number

6
Locker #

Build a Rain Forest in a Jar!

Puerto Rico has a rain forest. You can make your own rain forest.

WHAT YOU NEED:
- large glass jar with lid
- gravel or pebbles
- small plants
- soil
- water

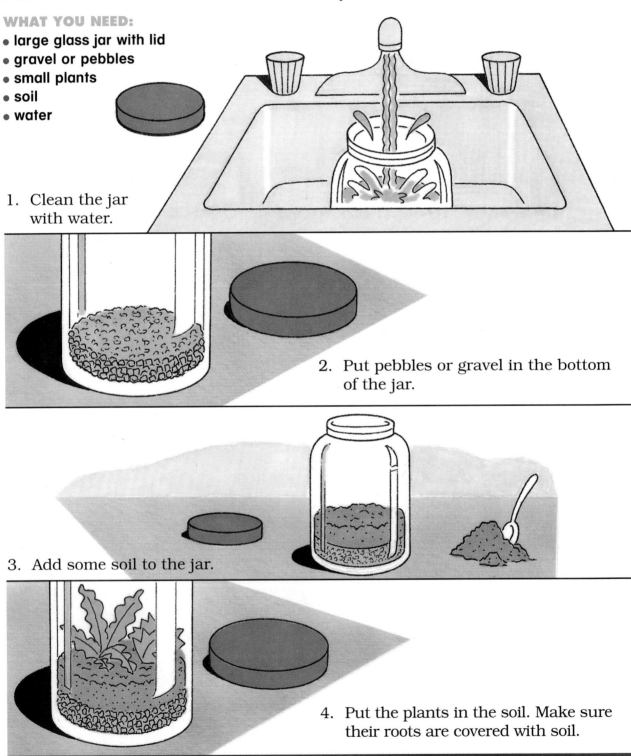

1. Clean the jar with water.

2. Put pebbles or gravel in the bottom of the jar.

3. Add some soil to the jar.

4. Put the plants in the soil. Make sure their roots are covered with soil.

5. Add enough water to make the soil damp, but not soggy.

6. Cover the jar so that air can't leak in or out.

7. Put the jar in a well-lit place, but not in direct sunlight.

   Watch your rain forest grow. Record your observations.

PUERTO RICO: THE FLOWER OF THE CARIBBEAN

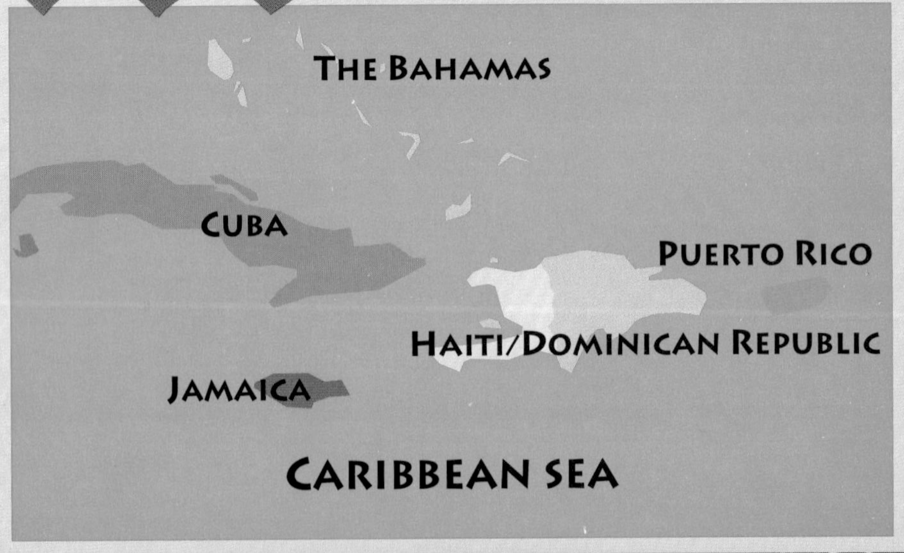

THE BAHAMAS

CUBA

PUERTO RICO

HAITI/DOMINICAN REPUBLIC

JAMAICA

CARIBBEAN SEA

Art Math Music
Science Social Studies
LANGUAGE ARTS

Puerto Rico is an island in the Caribbean Sea. Its nearest neighbors are Haiti and the Dominican Republic to the west and the Virgin Islands to the east. There are mountains, valleys, and plains. There is a beautiful rain forest. There are miles and miles of beaches in Puerto Rico. People like to go to the beach to swim or sit in the sun. The weather is warm all year, but rains come in the summer and fall. The dry season is December to March.

Puerto Rico was discovered by Columbus on his second voyage to the New World in 1493. He claimed it for Spain. Today, Puerto Rico is a commonwealth of the United States. Both English and Spanish are the main languages of Puerto Rico.

Most of the 3.8 million Puerto Ricans live in the cities. San Juan, the capital, is the largest city. Some people live in towns and villages in the mountains and along the coast.

Puerto Rico wants to host the Summer Olympic games in the year 2004. Baseball is one of the most popular sports in Puerto Rico. Many players from the United States play in the winter in Puerto Rico.

There are many festivals in Puerto Rico. Some are religious; some celebrate something special to a certain town. Festivals include crafts, music, dancing, and delicious food.

YOUR TURN Talk to a partner about where you are from. Take notes as you listen to your partner. Then tell the class about your partner's home country.

ALL STAR NEWS

"A good friend trusts you!"
Amal B., age 13, Miami, Florida

"A friend is someone you share secrets with."
Manuel H., age 12, Brownville, Texas

Teen Speak

WE ASKED SOME KIDS: WHAT MAKES A GOOD FRIEND? WHAT DO YOU THINK?

"Good friends talk on the phone with you. They let you play with their video games, too."
Jackie A., age 14, Los Angeles, California

Just Joking

What goes up and never goes down?

· · · · ·

Your age.

· · · · ·

Games

Zillions, a magazine for kids, took a poll about games. Almost 700 kids voted for their favorite games. Here are the best-liked board games. Did your favorite make the list?

Monopoly	**Outburst**	**Clue**
Taboo	**Life**	**Trivial Pursuit**
Risk	**Chess**	**Pictionary**

Take a poll in your school. Find out which games are most popular. Make a chart or graph.

Poetry Corner

Many colors
Black, white, copper like a penny,
toasted golden brown,
I am all of these.

Jennifer Chen

Art Math Music
Science Social Studies

LANGUAGE ARTS

News From All Over

Puerto Rico's Nature Reserve

El Faro is the name of Puerto Rico's nature reserve. El Faro is the Spanish word for "lighthouse." You probably have already guessed that there is a lighthouse in this reserve. There are also mangrove trees, a dry forest, rocky and sandy beaches, beds of turtle grass, and coral reefs.

El Faro has 316 acres. It is home to two endangered species: the manatee and the sea turtle.

AMAZING FACTS!

- In the United States, people own over 50 million dogs and 58 million cats!

- It takes 72 muscles to speak one word to a friend!

- More than 1 billion gallons of rain fall in the Puerto Rican rain forest each year.

Measuring Liberty

The Statue of Liberty was designed to make a big statement about freedom. Here are some of Liberty's measurements. How do they compare to yours?

Height: 152 ft.
Head: 28 ft.
Hand: 16 ft., 5 in.
Ear to ear: 20 ft.
Index finger: 8 ft.
Nose: 4 ft.

Original Americans

The very first Americans were hunters from Asia. They crossed into North America from Russia to Alaska by a land bridge that no longer exists.

HEY, THAT'S MINE!

People in many Native American Indian tribes made owner sticks to show that something belonged to them. Each person decorated their stick so that it was different from anyone else's.

Make an owner stick for yourself.

You need:
- Two sticks: One twelve inches long and one six inches long.
- Heavy twine
- Fun stuff to decorate your stick. Look at this one.

What you do:
1. Make a cross with the two sticks.
2. Wrap the twine around the sticks to hold them together and fasten them with a tight knot.
3. Decorate and make your stick one-of-a-kind.
4. Put your owner stick near something that belongs to you.

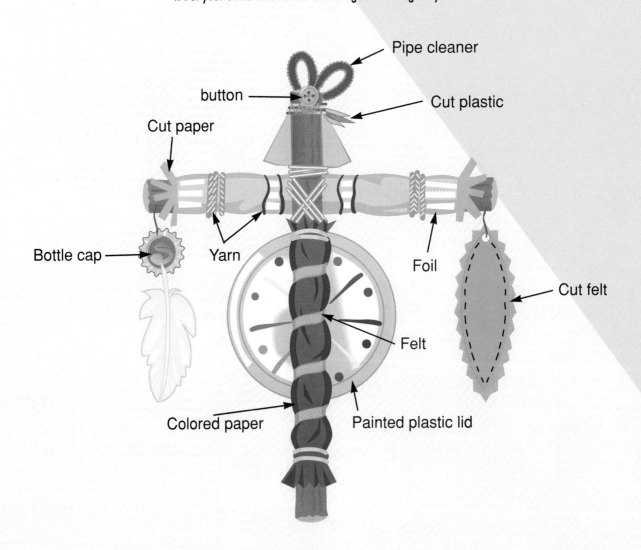

Pipe cleaner
button
Cut plastic
Cut paper
Bottle cap
Yarn
Foil
Cut felt
Felt
Colored paper
Painted plastic lid

Dear All Star News,
I like a girl in another grade. She is so smart and so nice. But I can't just go up to her and say, "Hi." How can I meet her?

Shy Sam

THEMEWORK TEAMWORK

1. **Make a poster.** Bring a photo of yourself to school. Glue it on a poster. What makes you proud? Write words under your photo. Share your poster with the class.

2. **Make a photo essay.** The story about Puerto Rico is called a photo essay. Make a photo essay of your country. You can use photos or cut out pictures from magazines. Read it to a partner.

3. **Use the Process Writing Portfolio.** Look in your portfolio for a list of ideas and writing topics related to this theme.

4. **Take a "favorite things" poll.** Ask your friends about their favorite things. Make a chart that looks like this:

Student	Clothes	Things to Do	Color	Sport	TV Show

Favorite Things

Meet José Ortiz

● ● ● ● ● ● ● ● ● ● ● ● ●

▶ LISTEN

1. How old is José?
   a. 15
   b. 11
   c. 20

2. Where is José from?
   a. Mexico
   b. Puerto Rico
   c. California

3. Where does he live now?
   a. Boston
   b. Houston
   c. New York

4. What does he like to do?
   a. play basketball
   b. shop at the mall
   c. watch TV

5. What does he eat at the mall?
   a. pizza and fried dough
   b. soup and salad
   c. hot dogs, ice cream, and pretzels

▶ SPEAK

Tell about José. What does he like to do? What doesn't he like to do?

Art   Math   Music
Science   Social Studies

L A N G U A G E   A R T S

READ

My mother paints beautiful pictures of houses and gardens. One of her paintings hangs at the mall. When I walk past it with my friends, I feel proud. My friends like my mother's painting.

My father is a carpenter in his spare time. He makes bird houses out of wood. Many people buy his bird houses. One day, I asked him to build a dog house for our dog, Hugo. But he said, "Hugo doesn't need a dog house. We want him to stay in the house where he's safe." He's right, but I still wish Hugo had a dog house.

WRITE

Write about yourself. What do you like to do? What don't you like to do?

THINK

What does José want his father to build? Do you think Hugo needs a dog house? Why or why not?

ONE BIG FAMILY

WORDS AND MUSIC BY BOB SCHNEIDER

Chorus
Everyone comes from a different place;
Everyone has a different face;
Everyone does different things you see—
But together we're one big family.

1st Verse
In Spanish hola means hello,
In Spanish hola means hello;
In Spanish hola means hello,
Hola means hello in Spanish.

Chorus

Art Math Music
Science Social Studies
LANGUAGE ARTS

Reading Corner

Try these terrific books!

The Emperor and the Kite
by Jane Yolen
A Chinese girl helps her father escape from a tower.

Journey To the Bright Kingdom
by Elizabeth Winthrop
A Japanese folktale about family love.

The Two-Thousand-Pound Goldfish
by Betty Byars
What do you do if your mother is wanted by the FBI?

IN MY MOTHER'S HOUSE

EXCERPTED FROM THE BOOK
BY ANN NOLAN CLARK

This story is about a Tewa Indian girl from New Mexico.

In my Mother's house
All day
I play and work;
All night
I sleep.

The walls come close around me
In a good way
I can see them;
I can feel them;
I live with them.

Art Math Music
Science Social Studies
LANGUAGE ARTS

This house is good to me,
It keeps me;
I like it,
My Mother's house.

...In my Mother's house
There is a fireplace:
The fireplace holds the fire.
On dark nights the fire is bright;
On cold nights the fire is warm.
The fire is always there,
To help me see,
To keep me warm.

In the plaza the people work;
In the plaza the people play
And sing and dance
And make ready for feasting.
It is the place
For all the people.

The plaza keeps the people together,
And the houses
With their backs to the mountains,
Stand facing the plaza
And shut it in.

My Mother's house,
It does not stand alone;
Its sister houses
Are all around it.

YOUR TURN Tell a partner about your house. What do you like about it? What do you like to do in your house?

Practice prepositions. Read the sentences below.

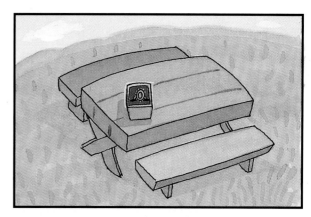

1. The basketball is **under** the hoop.
   The basketball is **on** the ground.

2. The ring is **in** the box.
   The ring is **on** the table.

3. The radio is **on** the table.
   The radio is **beside** the cake.

4. The ball is **beside** a chair.
   The ball is **between** a chair
   and a table.

5. The table is **between** the trees.
   The table is **under** the sky.

Art   Math   Music
Science   Social Studies

LANGUAGE ARTS

Describe the picture. Use *in*, *on*, *under*, *beside*, *and* *between* *as many times as you can. What do you think happened here?*

The Food Pyramid

To stay healthy, families need to eat the right foods. Look at the food pyramid. It shows the foods you need to eat each day. How many servings of each food do you eat every day?

Recommended Daily Servings

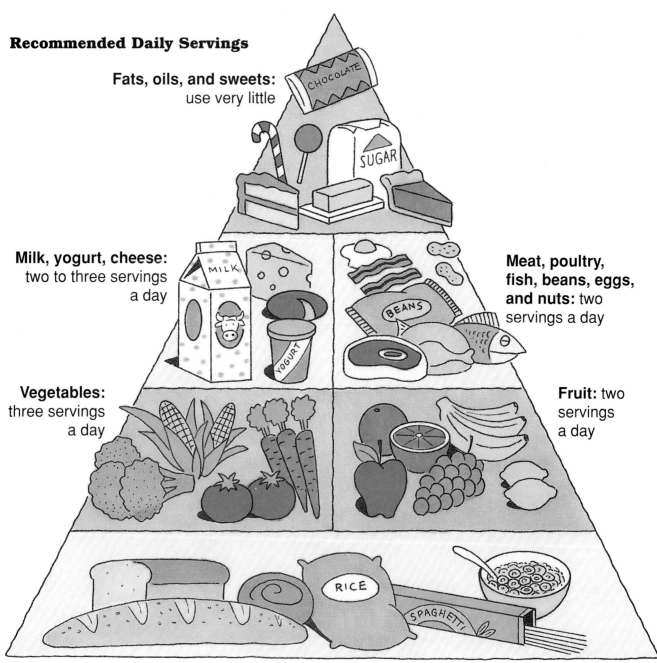

Fats, oils, and sweets: use very little

Milk, yogurt, cheese: two to three servings a day

Meat, poultry, fish, beans, eggs, and nuts: two servings a day

Vegetables: three servings a day

Fruit: two servings a day

Bread, cereal, rice, and pasta: six servings a day

Eat Yourself Healthy

Drink your milk. Get your share of calcium. Calcium builds strong bones. You can get calcium from milk, green vegetables, and fortified juices.

Say cheese, please. Certain cheeses can help prevent cavities! They eliminate acids in the mouth that can destroy teeth. Try Cheddar, American, Edam, or Gouda.

Get lots of vitamins. Oranges are rich in vitamin C. This vitamin may help protect against cataracts, an eye condition which often causes blindness. Over half of all Americans over the age of 75 get cataracts. So, plan ahead and protect your eyes now!

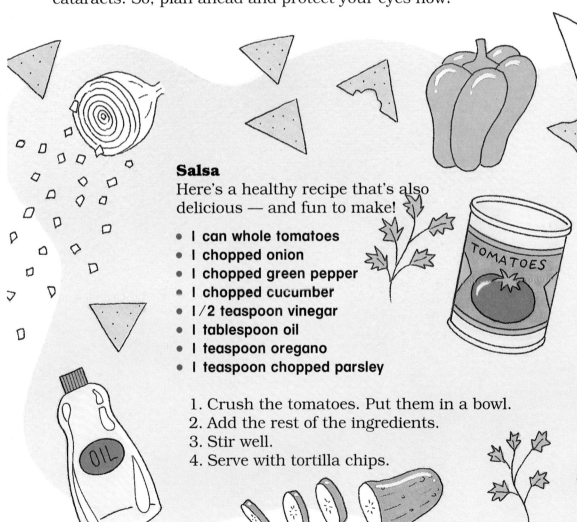

Salsa

Here's a healthy recipe that's also delicious — and fun to make!

- I can whole tomatoes
- I chopped onion
- I chopped green pepper
- I chopped cucumber
- I/2 teaspoon vinegar
- I tablespoon oil
- I teaspoon oregano
- I teaspoon chopped parsley

1. Crush the tomatoes. Put them in a bowl.
2. Add the rest of the ingredients.
3. Stir well.
4. Serve with tortilla chips.

INSIDE...

Many families play games and watch TV. Families read, study, and listen to music. Families cook, eat, wash dishes, and do laundry. What else do families do inside?

Bakery

MOVIES

Art Math Music
Science Social Studies

LANGUAGE ARTS

OUTSIDE...

Families wash windows, sweep steps, and empty trash. Families plant gardens, paint fences, and have barbeques. Families walk, swim, and ride bikes. What else do families do outside?

AROUND THE NEIGHBORHOOD...

Families are busy everywhere. Look around... at the supermarket, the dry cleaners, and the library ... at the hospital and the drugstore ... at restaurants and movie theaters ... at the hairdresser, the flower shop, and the bakery. Families are busy everywhere.

YOUR TURN Talk about the pictures with a partner. What do you see in each picture? Tell about your family, too.

My Bird Day

JANET S. WONG

When my grandfather says *birthday*
in his Chinese accent,
it sounds like "bird day,"
which is closer to truth—
for us, anyway.

At my birthday parties
we never have
paper streamers,
piñatas in trees,
balloons taped up
on the wall.
We decorate with platters
of peking duck,
soy sauce chicken and squab
in lettuce cups.
Food is all
that matters.

Other Chinese families
might do things
differently,
but my grandfather,
whose name is Duck,
thinks it's good
luck to make
a bird day
special.

Art   Math   Music
Science   Social Studies
LANGUAGE ARTS

The Dance

JOSÉ KAMHI

Look! A father and son are
flying kites together.
Watch them catch the wind!

Look, there they go!
Up, up
in a dance,
s
    o
      a
        r
          i
            n
              g

                g
             n
          i
        p
      o
    o
  w
s

down,
nearly hitting the ground.

Then up again,
the kites stop in the sky,
like hummingbirds in motion;
they don't move — then
Swoop down again.

YOUR TURN   Write your name in a soaring, swooping design.

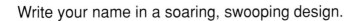

Art | Math | Music
Science | Social Studies
LANGUAGE ARTS

ALL STAR NEWS

Teen Speak

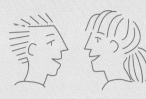

WE ASKED SOME KIDS: WHAT ARE YOU PROUD OF?

"I'm proud of myself! I study hard. I like to read. I get good grades. Math is my favorite subject."
Nadia C., age 12,
Springfield, Illinois

"I'm proud of my country. I come from Russia. Russians are brave. They are honest, too."
Alex P., age 15,
Newton, Massachusetts

"I'm proud of my school. We have a great basketball team. We have great teachers, too."
Terry G., age 13,
Yuma, Arizona

"I'm proud of my mother. She is a teacher. She is a great cook, too. She is smart and pretty. I love my mother."
Chris B., age 13,
Billings, Montana

Just Joking

Can you jump higher than my house?

¡dɯnɾ ʇ,uɐɔ sǝsnoH ˙ǝsɹnoɔ ɟO

Saturday Morning

We asked fifty kids what they did on Saturday morning. More than 80% watch Saturday morning cartoons on TV. Here are the rest of their top choices. What do you do on Saturday morning?

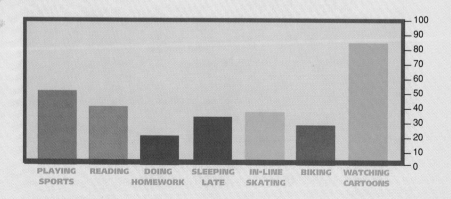

Art Math Music
Science Social Studies

Theme 2

LANGUAGE ARTS

News From All Over

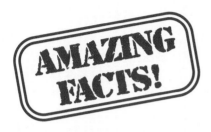

AMAZING FACTS!

- On Mother's Day, more than 103 million people make phone calls—most of them to a mom!

- The average American grown-up watches TV about four hours a day. The average American kid watches TV six and a half hours a day!

- Are you an average kid in an average American family? Then you will eat 1,500 peanut butter sandwiches by the time you're 18!

Movie Time

Does your family like to go to the movies? It can be very expensive. Long ago, theaters were called "nickelodeons." Can you guess why? Because it cost only a nickel to get in!

EVERY DAY IS SOMEBODY'S BIRTHDAY.
This chart shows you how many babies are born every day in an average week in the U.S.

Make a chart like this for your class.

SUNDAY	MONDAY	TUESDAY	WEDNESDAY	THURSDAY	FRIDAY	SATURDAY
8,532	10,243	10,730	10,515	10,476	10,525	8,799

PEN PALS

Find out more about families around the world. Join a pen pal club. There are lots of pen pal clubs. These clubs will match you up with kids in foreign countries. Some clubs are better than others. Here are the best ones:

CLUB	FEE	AGE YOU MUST BE	HOW TO JOIN
World Pen Pals 1694 Como Avenue St. Paul, MN 55108	$3 for 1 name	12-20	Write for an application. Enclose a stamped envelope addressed to you.
Student Letter Exchange 630 Third Avenue New York, NY 10017	$6 for 3 names	8-17	Same as above.
Afro-Asian Center PO Box 337 Saugerties, NY 12477	$1 for 1 name	10-17	Write a letter that tells your interests, age, and which country you want. Send $1 and a stamped envelope addressed to you.

LETTER-WRITING TIPS

1. Write about everyday stuff. What may seem boring to you may be really interesting to a pen pal in another country.

2. Send pictures of yourself, your family, your friends.

3. Other stuff to send: stickers, stamps, postcards, magazine articles, etc.

4. Ask your pen pal about favorite stars, sports, movies, etc.

5. Tell jokes. Write special poems.

Dear All Star News,

In my class, two students make fun of me. They make fun of my clothes and the way I talk. I try to speak good English, but I make mistakes. Please help me. I want them to stop teasing me.

Feeling the Blues

THEMEWORK TEAMWORK

1. **Make a photo essay.** Make a photo essay of your family. Write some sentences about each picture. Tell the class about your photo essay.

2. **Research.** Find out more about the Tewa Indians of New Mexico. Work with a partner. Your teacher will help you.

3. **Use the Process Writing Portfolio.** Look in your portfolio for a list of ideas and writing topics related to this theme.

4. **Take a families poll.** Ask your friends about their families. Make a chart that looks like this.

F A M I L I E S

Student	Mother's Name	Father's Name	How Many Brothers/ Sisters	Brothers'/ Sisters' Ages	Brothers'/ Sisters' Names

Mike's Problem

● ● ● ● ● ● ● ● ● ● ● ●

▶ **LISTEN**

Listen to the beginning of the story. Then choose the best answer.

1. What does Mike like to do after school?
   a. go to the library
   b. go home and eat
   c. go ice skating

2. What did he do yesterday?
   a. He went to meet Maria.
   b. He went home.
   c. He went skating with his friends.

3. What was wrong with Mike?
   a. He was hungry and tired.
   b. He was sick.
   c. He was lonesome for Maria.

4. What did his mother do?
   a. Called the doctor.
   b. Called Mike's father.
   c. Came to get Mike at school.

▶ **SPEAK**

Tell about Mike. What was his problem?
What did he have to do?
Why did this upset him?

40

▶ READ

At home, Mike got into bed. His mother brought him a glass of soda to drink and told him to try to sleep. A few hours later, Mike woke up. He felt better, but he still had a fever. His mother gave him a bowl of chicken soup and some crackers. After he ate, Mike called Maria.

"Maria, this is Mike."

"Hi, Mike! Where were you this afternoon? I looked for you when I went skating, but I didn't see you."

"I'm sorry, Maria. I couldn't meet you because I have the flu."

"Oh, no," said Maria. "I hope you feel better soon."

"Me, too," said Mike.

"The skating competition is tomorrow. Do you think you'll feel well enough to go?"

"I don't know. My mother won't let me go if I have a fever."

"If you can't go, I'll tell you all about it.

"Thanks, Maria."

Mike hung up the phone. He was smiling.

"I guess you're feeling better," said his mother.

"Yes," said Mike. "Maria is a good friend."

▶ WRITE

What does Mike want to do after school tomorrow? Write a letter to Mike about what you like to do after school.

▶ THINK

How did Mike feel after he talked to Maria? Was he happy or sad? Why? Why is Maria a good friend?

WHEN IS YOUR BIRTHDAY

WORDS AND MUSIC BY ANDY VALLARIO AND LARRY MILTON

Hey, hey. When is your birthday?
Can you tell me the day, the month, the year?
We'd like to know about your birthday.
We'll have a party
Do happy things
Blow out the candles as we dance and sing.

Please, please. Talk about your birthday.
Does it come in the winter, spring, summer, or fall?
We'd like to know about your birthday.

Is it in January?
February?
March or April, May, June or July?
Is it in August?
September?
October? November?
Or maybe in December?

Hey, hey. When is your birthday?
Can you tell me the day when you were born?

Getting Along Together

Reading Corner

Try these terrific books!

What's the Opposite of a Best Friend?
by A. Bates
Two girls have problems growing up.

The Toilet Paper Tigers
by Gordon Korman
A baseball team tries to get it together.

Who Ran My Underwear Up the Flagpole?
by Jerry Spinelli
Four misfits suddenly score big during the football season.

A Win for Sung Hee

Hello, I am Sung Hee Choung. I am Korean-American. I go to Sunny Brooke Junior High. My brother, Doo Jin, goes to the same school. He is in the ninth grade. I am in the seventh grade. He is tall and strong. I am tall and strong, too. Doo Jin is a champion Ping-Pong player. I like baseball. I play first base. I love to hit the ball.

I'm Doo Jin. Sung Hee wants to play on the school's baseball team. But no girls can play. Only boys can play. The coach says, "Girls? Girls? We don't want girls on our team." I think the coach is wrong.

Art | Math | Music
Science | Social Studies
LANGUAGE ARTS

The coach doesn't want me. But I'm going to the tryouts anyway. I can hit the ball better than the boys. I'm going to do my best. I'm not going to give up.

Sung Hee is at the tryouts. Doo Jin and his friend Roberto are watching. Sung Hee feels nervous. Her heart is beating really fast. She takes a deep breath. She swings at a pitch...crack! She hits the ball. The ball goes over the fence. It's a home run!

Sung Hee plays first base. A batter hits the ball on the ground. Sung Hee fields the ball. She throws to home plate. The runner is out!

Your sister really IS better than the boys. I think the coach will pick her.

 YOUR TURN   Can girls play sports as well as boys? Talk about it with a partner.

I Love Baseball

WENDY WATANABE

I love the fans,
the smell of peanuts...
Vendors shout, "Get your hot dogs; get your hot dogs here!"
The flag, the national anthem....
The umpire shouts, "Play ball!"
The fans cheer; the players take the field.
Let the game begin!

A

Regular present verbs:

eat	eats	teach	teaches
play	plays	go	goes
walk	walks	watch	watches
ride	rides	practice	practices
sleep	sleeps	wash	washes
clean	cleans	write	writes

Listen first. Look at the pictures. Then read the sentences.

What does she do every week?

1. She rides her bike to work.
2. She goes to the bank.
3. She plays soccer.
4. She teaches at a daycare center.

What do they do every week?

1. They ride the bus to work.
2. They go to the store.
3. They play tennis.
4. They teach at a high school.

Theme 3

LANGUAGE ARTS

Ask questions. Answer the questions. Use the chart.

What do they do on Sunday?
They play golf.

What does he do on...? Wednesday?
he Practices drums.

What does she do on ...? Monday
She goes to a dance lesson.

What does it do on ...? Saturday
The dog chases a cat.

	Sunday	Monday	Tuesday	Wednesday	Thursday	Friday	Saturday
	play golf	walk to work	ride the bus	teach a class	wash the floor	go to the bank	watch a movie
	watches TV	goes to the library	plays baseball	practices drums	washes his clothes	eats ice cream	cleans his room
	reads a book	goes to a dance lesson	writes a letter	plays basketball	goes to the mall	walks the dog	rides her bike
	sleeps	eats	sleeps	eats	sleeps	eats	chases a cat

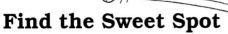
Find the Sweet Spot

Find the "sweet spot" on a baseball bat.
The sweet spot is where the bat hits the ball best.

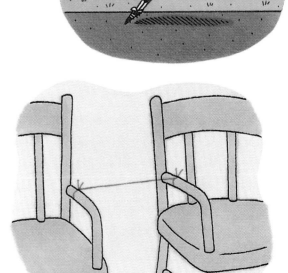

WHAT YOU NEED:
- 2 chairs with arms
- string
- a piece of wood $\frac{3}{4}$" thick
  and about 2" wide and 24" long
- salt
- pencil
- cork

1. Put the chairs about 12" apart.

2. Stretch the string from one arm to the other arm.

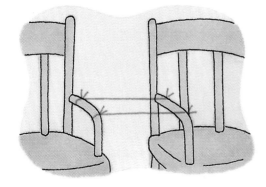

3. Stretch another string.

4. Lay the wood on the strings.

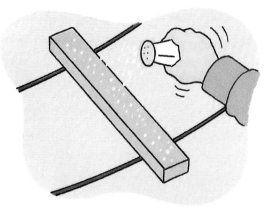

5. Shake salt all over the wood.

6. Push the cork onto the end of the pencil.

7. Tap the wood with the cork.

8. Keep tapping. Make the wood vibrate.

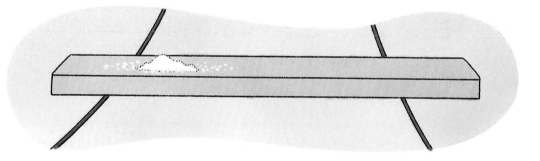

9. See where the salt gathers on the wood. This is the sweet spot.

The wood does not vibrate at the sweet spots. A sweet spot on a bat doesn't vibrate either. Think about where this spot might be on a bat. Hit the ball at this spot and you may be the next Home Run Champion!

LET'S PLAY SOCCER!

Soccer is a popular sport in many countries. Boys and girls of all ages play soccer. Do you play soccer? Do you want to learn?

First, you need two teams of 11 people. Each team tries to get the ball across the field to the opposite goal. To score a point, you must kick the ball past the goalkeeper and into the net. It's that easy! Boys and girls can run, pass, kick, and have a great time.

Art | Math | Music
Science | Social Studies

LANGUAGE ARTS

Here's how to kick a soccer ball. Put one foot next to the ball. Swing the other leg toward the ball. Point your toes and hit the ball with the side of your foot. Let your kicking leg continue swinging in the direction you want the ball to go.

Goalkeepers are the only players who can touch the ball with their hands when it's in play. Other players use their feet, legs, bodies, or heads to hit the ball.

Heading is a great way to pass the ball when it comes at you through the air. Hit the ball with your forehead, but be careful!

54

Soccer Talk

Dribble
Kick the ball along the ground while running.

Tackle
Use your feet to take the ball away from an opponent.

Pass
Kick the ball to your team members. Remember—no hands!

Mark
Guard the ball and make it hard for an opponent to get it.

Foul
When a player breaks a rule.

Fake
Pretend to kick or pass the ball. Then do something different.

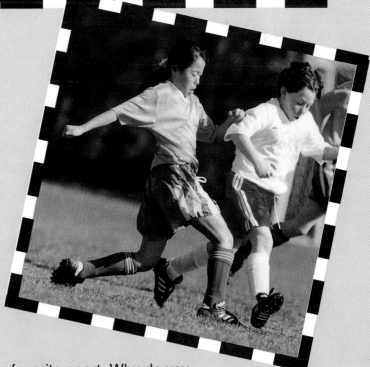

 YOUR TURN Tell a partner about your favorite sport. Why do you like this sport? Talk about your partner's favorite sport.

ALL STAR NEWS

Teen Speak

WE ASKED SOME KIDS: HOW DO YOU GET YOUR SPENDING MONEY?

"I have a paper route. Every afternoon I deliver the newspaper to the houses on my list. The newspaper office pays me $12 at the end of the week."

Cary M., age 14,
Grafton, Massachusetts

"I get an allowance of $5 a week. I make my bed every morning and take out the trash when it's full. On Saturday mornings, I clean my room."

Abdul H., age 12,
Seattle, Washington

"After school, I help my dad in his store. I sweep the floors and stack boxes. Sometimes I help a customer find something. My dad pays me $3.00 an hour."

Raoul P., age 15,
Detroit, Michigan

"My friend's family runs a riding stable. They need lots of help taking care of the horses. I work there after school on Wednesdays and on Saturday mornings. I earn $15 a week."

Selena G., age 13,
Miami, Florida

What Kids Buy

- Most kids buy fun "extras" such as games, toys, sports items, snacks, music, jewelry, and movie tickets.
- One in three kids older than eleven buys clothes or shoes.
- Many kids save some money every week.
- What about you and your friends?

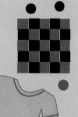

Bank Book

Just Joking

Where do swimmers eat lunch?

At pool tables.

Art | Math | Music
Science | Social Studies

LANGUAGE ARTS

News From All Over

SPORTS TEAMS AND THEIR NAMES

AMAZING FACTS!

- Track athletes are most likely to break records late in the day when their body temperatures are highest.
- Olympic athletes work hard to win gold medals. But, guess what? The gold medals are made mostly of silver. Only about 0.2 ounces of pure gold coats the outside of the medal.

Hundreds of professional and amateur sports teams use Native American Indian names. Many Native Americans don't like it. Native Americans protested at the 1995 World Series between the Atlanta Braves and the Cleveland Indians. The protesters objected to the team names, the team mascots, and the team symbols—tomahawks, bows and arrows, and feather headdresses. They say that use of these things dishonors their culture. Other Americans disagree. They don't see anything wrong with using Native American Indian names or symbols.

In the town of Mukwonago, Wisconsin, the high school's football team is "The Mukwonago Indians." The town held a hearing about the team's name. Students voted 410 to 32 to keep the name.

What's your opinion? Should sports teams use Native American names? Why or why not?

Bright Ideas

YOUNG INVENTORS HELP OTHERS

Kids in Bothell, Washington, read about a "surf chair" that allows people in wheelchairs to go to the beach and into shallow water.

Students at Spiritridge School decided to build an "all-terrain chair" for their classmates in wheelchairs. They called the company that made the "surf chair" for ideas. They also called wheelchair manufacturers, hardware, plumbing, motorcycle, golf, bicycle, and dune buggy stores!

First, they built a model out of Tinkertoys, straws, and ice cream sticks. Next, they made scale drawings. Then, they followed the drawings and used PVC pipe, a metal base frame, and wheelbarrow wheels. They added a beach umbrella, colorful cushions, and a shoulder harness. The wheelchair was ready to roll. Now, a student in an "all-terrain chair" can wheel right up to home plate and get a hit!

Poetry Corner

A person smiles,
Another smiles in return,
And soon...
Everyone smiles.

Mitsuyo Aoyagi, Grade 6
P.S. 201, Queens, New York

Dear All Star News,
I get an allowance, but every week I spend all my money. How can I save money?

J.R.

THEMEWORK TEAMWORK

1. **Make a photo essay.** Choose your favorite sport, or choose your favorite star in sports. Write a photo essay. Share your essay with a partner.

2. **Take a sports poll.** Ask ten friends, "What is your least favorite sport? Why?" Make a chart that looks like this.

STUDENT	LEAST FAVORITE SPORT	WHY?

3. **Make a bar graph.** Make a bar graph from your poll results. Your teacher will help you. Compare your bar graph with other students' bar graphs.

4. **Use the Process Writing Portfolio.** Look in your portfolio for a list of ideas and writing topics related to this theme.

Bonnie Blair, A Champion on Ice

 LISTEN

1. What does Bonnie love to do?
   a. skate
   b. bicycle
   c. swim
2. Where did she grow up?
   a. Canada
   b. Illinois
   c. Puerto Rico
3. What did she compete in?
   a. cheerleading
   b. tennis
   c. skating races
4. What decision did she make?
   a. to devote her life to skating
   b. to do extra things at school
   c. to stop skating

 SPEAK

Tell about Bonnie Blair. What does she like to do? What big decision did she have to make?

Art Math Music
Science Social Studies
LANGUAGE ARTS

READ

Bonnie Blair is an Olympic champion now. She has won five gold medals for speed skating. She has won more gold medals than any other woman athlete in history. Only four American men have won more Olympic gold medals than Bonnie.

But, Bonnie doesn't just love to win medals, she loves to skate. Many people think this is the secret to her success. She skates every race the same way. She tries to win, but she's never sure she will win until she crosses the finish line.

There is a street named after Bonnie in her hometown of Champaign, Illinois. It's called Bonnie Blair Drive. Many people admire Bonnie and feel proud of her.

At age 30, Bonnie retired from competition. She wants to get married and have children. She also wants to coach teenage skaters. Maybe one of them will go to the Olympics, too.

WRITE
How many medals did Bonnie win? What is her secret? Write about it.

THINK
Why do you think her hometown named a street after her? How do people feel about Bonnie?

NO, NO, NO

WORDS AND MUSIC BY BOB SCHNEIDER

Shelly, Shelly, Shelly, got tickets to the show!
No, no, no, don't want to go.
Shelly, Shelly, Shelly, they're in the front row!
Maybe, maybe, baby, don't really know.
I say, Shelly, Shelly, Shelly, the band is the best!
Yes, yes, yes, oh what a mess —
Things can be so crazy when you can't make up your mind — I said

Chorus
No, no, no, don't want to go,
Maybe, maybe, baby, don't really know;
Yes, yes, yes, oh what a mess!
Things can be so crazy when you can't make up your mind!

Kerry, Kerry, Kerry, want to go to the game?
No, no, no, don't want to go.
Kerry, Kerry, Kerry, your favorite team is playing!
Maybe, maybe, baby, don't really know.
Kerry, Kerry, Kerry, the team is the best!
Yes, yes, yes, oh what a mess —
Things can be so crazy when you can't make up your mind — I said

Chorus

Art Math Music
Science Social Studies

LANGUAGE ARTS

HOPES AND DREAMS

Reading Corner

Try these terrific books!

Of Swans, Sugarplums and Satin Slippers
by Violette Verdy
Great art and beautiful ballet stories.

Uncle Jed's Barbershop
by Margaree King Mitchell
A story of hope from the segregated South in the 1920's.

B-Ball: The Team That Never Lost a Game
by Ron Jones
A great, true story of the San Francisco Special Olympics basketball team.

AFRICA DREAM

ELOISE GREENFIELD

I went all the way to Africa
In a dream one night
I crossed over the ocean
In a slow, smooth jump.

And landed in Africa
Long-ago Africa

I went to the city
And shopped in the marketplace
For pearls and perfume

With magic eyes
I read strange words
In old books
And understood

I leaned small against
Tall stone buildings

Art Math Music
Science Social Studies

LANGUAGE ARTS

And rode through the crowds
On a donkey's back

I dreamed I went to Africa
Long-ago Africa
I went to a village
And stood lonesome-still...

Till my long-ago granddaddy
With my daddy's face
Stretched out his arms
And welcomed me home

He knelt on one knee
And planted one seed
That grew into ten tall trees
With mangoes for me

I danced a hello dance
To the drums of my uncles

And sang a hello song
In a circle with new-old friends

I walked with my cousins
All over Africa
Lifting my long dress
To step across countries

66

And when I got tired
I turned into a baby
And my long-ago grandma
With Mama's face
Held me in her arms
And rocked me
Rocked me
To sleep

YOUR TURN Do you dream about a place of long-ago? Where is that place? Talk to a partner about it. Then share your dream with another pair of classmates.

Hopes and Dreams

A

Regular past verbs:		Irregular past verbs:	
dream	dreamed	come	came
jump	jumped	speak	spoke
		get	got
		write	wrote

I dreamed I was an animal trainer in the circus. I lived a great life. I traveled across the country. I stayed in the best hotels. My fans loved me and my animals. They cheered when the lions danced. They clapped when the tigers jumped through hoops. They whistled and stamped their feet when the act was over. It was a great dream. I wonder what being an animal trainer is really like.

★ Did she dream she was a doctor?
● No, she didn't.
★ What did she dream?
● She dreamed she was an animal trainer.

***Read the story. Then answer the questions on a
separate piece of paper.***

I dreamed I was in English class. Principal Mason came
into the classroom. He spoke to the whole class. He said,
"Miss Diaz is sick." Then he pointed to me and said, "Harold,
you have to be the teacher." The principal looked at the
students and told them to be good. Then he walked out of
the room.

I felt scared, but I walked to the front of the room. I
opened the teacher's desk and I got some chalk. I wrote some
math problems on the board. I started to explain the
problems. The students didn't listen to me. They talked and
laughed.

I felt so angry! I called Principal Mason. He answered
the phone. Then I woke up.

1. Who came to the classroom? *Principal mason*
2. What did Principal Mason say to the class?
3. What did he say to Harold?
4. What did the principal tell the students?
5. How did Harold feel when he walked to the
   front of the room?
6. Where did he get the chalk?
7. What did he write on the board?
8. What did the students do?
9. Was this story real? *NO*
   How do you know? *Because it was a Dream*

Chippewa Dream Catcher

The Chippewa make dream catchers from wooden hoops with webs and feathers. Bad dreams get caught in the web. Good dreams float through the web and down the feathers into the sleeper's mind.

WHAT YOU NEED:

- a white paper plate
- 12 inches of yarn
- beads
- feathers
- masking tape, pencil, scissors

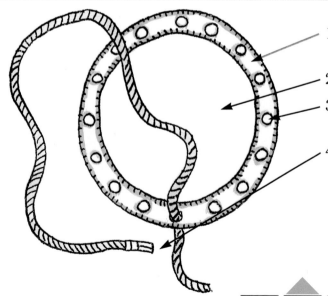

1. Draw a large ring inside the rim of the paper plate.

2. Cut out the center of the plate.

3. Punch about 16 holes around the ring.

4. Wrap masking tape around one end of the yarn. Poke the taped end through a hole and pull through, leaving about 3 inches at the end.

Art Math Music
Science Social Studies
LANGUAGE ARTS

5. Begin creating the web by crisscrossing the yarn through the rest of the holes in the ring. Leave the center open.

6. Take the taped end of the yarn back to the first hole and tie it to the loose, 3-inch end.

7. Cut a piece of yarn about 8 inches long. Loop it through a hole opposite the first hole. Pass several beautiful beads up the yarn. Add a feather or two, and knot the end of the yarn.

8. Share your dream catcher with your friends. Then hang it over your bed. Sweet dreams!

Hopes and Dreams

The Magic of Dance

Jacques d'Amboise was a very famous dancer. He was the main dancer for the New York City Ballet for many years. Later, he became a teacher and started the NDI—National Dance Institute. He wanted to teach kids the magic of dance.

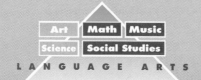

Art Math Music
Science Social Studies
LANGUAGE ARTS

"NDI taught me to achieve, to fulfill my dreams. It taught me that there should be no limit to dreams. I can become whoever and whatever I want to be in life."
-Peter Fong.

In 1976, NDI was in only four New York City schools, and reached only 80 kids. Today, NDI reaches thousands of kids from ages 8 to 14 every year. There are classes, workshops, scholarships, and performances. The most famous performance is called The Event of the Year. Every June, more than 1,000 kids all dance together.

More than 80% of NDI dancers are black, Hispanic, or Asian. Some are homeless. Some are blind. Some are slow learners. But they all love to dance.

"NDI taught me to look up, lift my feet and believe in myself."
—Emilio Sanchez.

But NDI isn't just about dancing. It's about lots of practice, hard work and sweat. It's about cooperation and working together. It's about believing in yourself and pride.

"I dreamed of being in NDI," says Oya Bangura. "NDI is like finding an open door in life."

YOUR TURN   What is your dream? Talk to a partner about your favorite activities.

I Have a Dream

MARTIN LUTHER KING, JR.

I have a dream
That one day this nation will rise up
And live out the true meaning of its creed;
"We hold these truths to be self-evident,
That all men are created equal."

I have a dream
That one day on the red hills of Georgia
The sons of former slaves
And the sons of former slave-owners
Will be able to sit down together
At the table of brotherhood.

I have a dream
That my four little children
Will one day live in a nation
Where they will not be judged
By the color of their skin
But by the content of their character.

(excerpted from a speech in Washington, D.C., 1963)

YOUR TURN What does the writer hope will happen in the future? This speech was written over 30 years ago. Has the writer's dream come true? Why or why not? Talk about it with your class and the teacher.

Hopes and Dreams

ALL STAR NEWS

Teen Speak

WE ASKED KIDS: IF YOU COULD HAVE ONE DREAM COME TRUE, WHAT WOULD IT BE?

"I'd help homeless people get food and safe places to sleep."
Ben F., age 14,
Chicago, Illinois

"My dream is to become an Olympic champion. I practice four hours a day to help make my dream come true."
Karen L., age 12,
Denver, Colorado

"I dream of being back home in the Dominican Republic. My grandparents still live there and I miss them very much."
Joseph B., age 11,
Philadelphia, Pennsylvania

Just Joking

Why was the basketball coach in outer space?

▸▸▸▸▸

He was looking for an all-star team!

◂◂◂◂◂

Dream Job

Here are the top ten professions that teens hope to enter when they are adults. What is your dream job?

- DOCTOR
- MOVIE STAR
- ASTRONAUT
- LAWYER
- PROFESSIONAL ATHLETE
- PROFESSIONAL MUSICIAN
- DENTIST
- TEACHER
- SOFTWARE DEVELOPER
- ARTIST

Poetry Corner

In South Carolina
There is a big house with a yard
A dark room.
A bed with no one in it
Mine.

Denise Chamberlain
Queens, New York

News From All Over

What's So Special?

Kelly Ann Kettles is a gymnast. She performs her floor exercises like a ballet dancer. Her routine on the uneven bars is flawless. She treats the vault like a bump in the rug.

"Piece of cake," said Kelly after a great dismount. "It's amazing what training can do!"

Why is Kelly so special? She has only been training for five years. And like 7.5 million other Americans, she was born mentally retarded.

Like the "regular" Olympics, the Special Olympics awards ribbons and medals. But at the Special Olympics, winning isn't important. Trying is important. Sharing the experience is important. Friendships are important. The Special Olympics help each athlete believe that no obstacle is too high to jump and no race is too far to run.

AMAZING FACTS!

- Robots are not new inventions. The Chinese people dreamed them up 750 years ago.

- The world's largest table was set up in Spain in 1986. It was nearly a mile long and had seats for 6,400 people!

- The human brain contains an estimated 100 billion cells. It is the most complex object in the universe.

KID PHOTOS

Maybe you're dreaming of becoming a famous photographer. **Shooting Back** is a photography program for city kids. It helps kids express themselves through photography. Adult volunteers teach kids how to use a camera and develop their own film. The photographers keep journals and write about their photos, too. Below are photos taken by kids in Washington, D.C. and Minneapolis, Minnesota.

Tips for Taking Good Photos

1. RELAX. The camera is a friendly tool.

2. THINK BEFORE YOU SHOOT. What do you want to show in the photo?

3. LOOK FOR NEW AND DIFFERENT ANGLES TO SHOOT FROM. Take a photo from your knees or from up high.

4. ASK PERMISSION TO TAKE SOMEONE'S PICTURE FIRST.

5. AS YOU AIM, TAKE A DEEP BREATH. Exhale as you snap the photo. One last thing: Don't forget to take the lens cap off!

UNICEF

Since 1950, kids in the U.S. have raised more than 100 million dollars for UNICEF.

UNICEF is the United Nations' agency that gives help to children around the world. If your class wants to help, write to:

UNICEF
PO Box 182248
Chattanooga, TN 37422-7248

Dear All Star News,

I have a job after school. Then I do all my homework after dinner. My mother works at night, so I take care of my two brothers. I'm so tired, I fall into bed at night. But sometimes I can't get to sleep. I toss and turn in my bed. The next morning, I feel terrible. I can hardly stay awake in class some days. How can I get to sleep?

Sleepy Sue

THEMEWORK TEAMWORK

1. **Create a dream story.** "Africa Dream" is a fantasy about the writer's family history. Make your own homeland dream story about your family history. Draw or find pictures to illustrate it. Read your story to a partner.

2. **Create a photo essay.** The "Magic of Dance" is a photo essay. Do you like to dance? Sing? Play a musical instrument? Make your own photo essay about a favorite activity.

3. **Take a poll.** Ask ten friends about their futures. What do they hope to be? Why? Make a chart that looks like this.

Name	Future Career	Why I Dream of It	How I Can Reach My Goal

Compare your results with your classmates. Then make one big chart of all the results from your class.

4. **Use the Process Writing Portfolio.** Look in your portfolio for ideas and writing topics related to this theme.

Martin Luther King, Jr.
●●●●●●●●●●●●●●●●

▶ LISTEN

1. What did Martin Luther King, Jr. study to be?
   a. a teacher
   b. a minister
   c. a lion tamer

2. What did Rosa Parks do on the bus?
   a. stood in the back of the bus
   b. sat in the back of the bus
   c. sat in the front of the bus

3. What happened to Rosa Parks?
   a. she was arrested
   b. she got off the bus
   c. she met a friend

4. What did Martin Luther King, Jr. do?
   a. rode the buses
   b. warned African Americans not to sit in the front of the bus
   c. led a peaceful protest

▶ SPEAK

Tell what happened in Montgomery, Alabama.

Art   Math   Music
Science   Social Studies
LANGUAGE ARTS

Theme **4**

READ

It was not easy for the African Americans to give up riding the buses. For most of them, the buses were their only way to travel around the city. They walked, hitchhiked, rode in car pools — even in horse-drawn wagons — and the buses stayed empty. King and his supporters were threatened. King's house was destroyed by a bomb. But still, the buses were empty. At last, the bus company gave in, and the law was changed. Martin Luther King, Jr. had won his first protest peacefully.

King led protests and demonstrations all over the country during the next few years. Everywhere he went, he talked about love, patience, and most of all, non-violence. He believed that African Americans could win their struggle for equal rights without violence. Millions of people all over the world knew about King and his beliefs. He was both admired and hated.

In 1964, Martin Luther King, Jr. won the Nobel Peace Prize. He was only thirty-four years old — the youngest man to ever receive this high honor.

WRITE

What is your dream for a better world? Write about it. Start with, "I have a dream that one day..."

THINK

"We must learn to live together as brothers, or we will perish together as fools...," said Martin Luther King, Jr. Think about what these words mean.

Hopes and Dreams

WHEN YOU DREAM A DREAM

WORDS AND MUSIC BY BOB SCHNEIDER

Chorus
When you dream a dream,
What do you find?
When you dream a dream,
What do you see?
When you dream a dream,
Where do you go?
When you dream a dream,
Let your feelings flow.

I dreamed I was a queen,
Sitting on my throne;
I dreamed I was a king or queen,
And I was not alone.

Chorus

I dreamed I was a singer,
Singing for my friends;
I dreamed I was a singer,
And it would never end.

Chorus

NEW FACES, NEW PLACES

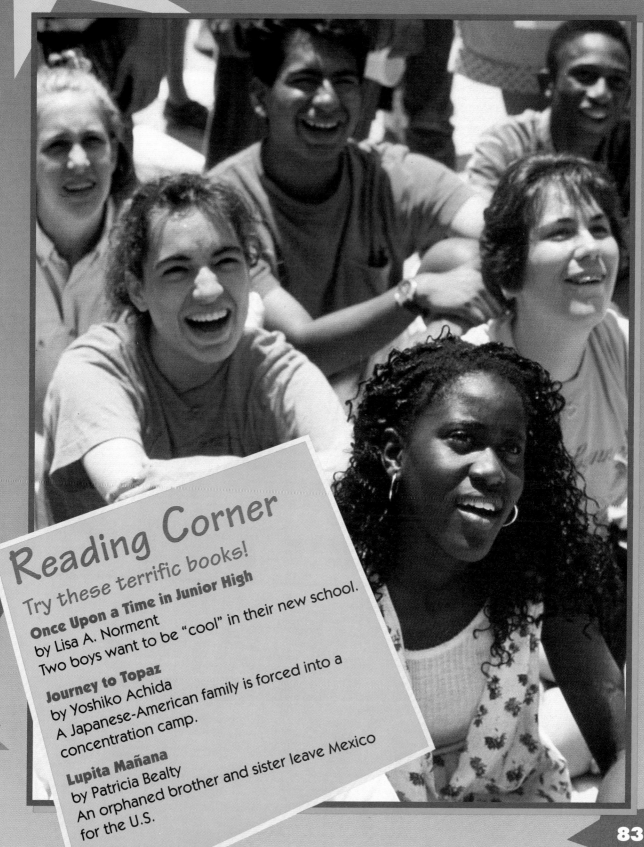

Reading Corner

Try these terrific books!

Once Upon a Time in Junior High
by Lisa A. Norment
Two boys want to be "cool" in their new school.

Journey to Topaz
by Yoshiko Achida
A Japanese-American family is forced into a concentration camp.

Lupita Mañana
by Patricia Bealty
An orphaned brother and sister leave Mexico for the U.S.

The Family from Vietnam

ADAPTED FROM THE BOOK BY TANA REIFF

About the story

TIME: 1975, after the Vietnam War

PLACE: The United States

MAIN CHARACTERS:
Mai, a refugee woman from Vietnam
Set, Mai's husband
Bao and Thi, Mai and Set's children
Mr. and Mrs. Baker, sponsors for Mai and her children

SETTING THE SCENE:
A family from Vietnam is separated after the war.
The mother and children come to the United States.

Part 1

The Job

Life in Lancaster was very difficult for Mai. She was poor. She had no husband. She had no job. She was living in an American city. It was a long way from her little village in Vietnam.

Mr. and Mrs. Baker were very good to Mai. They helped her a lot. Still, Mai wanted to be able to do things for herself. She didn't think she would ever see Set again.

Mai was a very smart woman. She did many things with her time. She went to school. She learned a lot. She put ads in the Vietnamese newspapers in the United States. She hoped the ads would help find her husband.

Art Math Music
Science Social Studies
LANGUAGE ARTS

Soon she started to look for a job. In schools she had learned how to fill out a job application. She learned how to use a bus. And Mr. Baker sometimes took her in his car to look for jobs. But it was hard.

"Mr. Baker," she said. "I want to work. You are very good to me, but I should work. I will take any job."

She found an ad in the newspaper for a job at a chicken farm. She wanted to work, so Mr. Baker took her there.

"This is not very clean work," said the man at the chicken farm. "We kill chickens here. Then we get them ready to sell. But if you want a job helping us, you can have it."

"I want the job," said Mai.

"OK, then it's yours," the man answered.

Mai started work the next day.

The Letter

The man was right. It wasn't very nice work. But it wasn't too bad. Mai was making enough money to live on. This was what she had wanted. Yet something was missing.

Every day she thought of her home in Vietnam. She could never forget how pretty the village had been before the war. The war had made the country so ugly. She missed home. "I wonder if Set is still there," she thought. "I wonder if he is still alive."

One day Mai got home from work late in the afternoon. The children were playing. She was glad they were doing so well. They learned English very fast. They made friends with American children. She heard them laughing outside.

She went to see if she had any mail. No letters. Wait—there was a letter way in the back of the box. She pulled it out and looked at it. She knew the writing. It was Set's writing!

"**B**ao! Thi! Come here! There's a letter from your father!"
It had been a year since Mai had seen that writing. She read the letter out loud to the children.

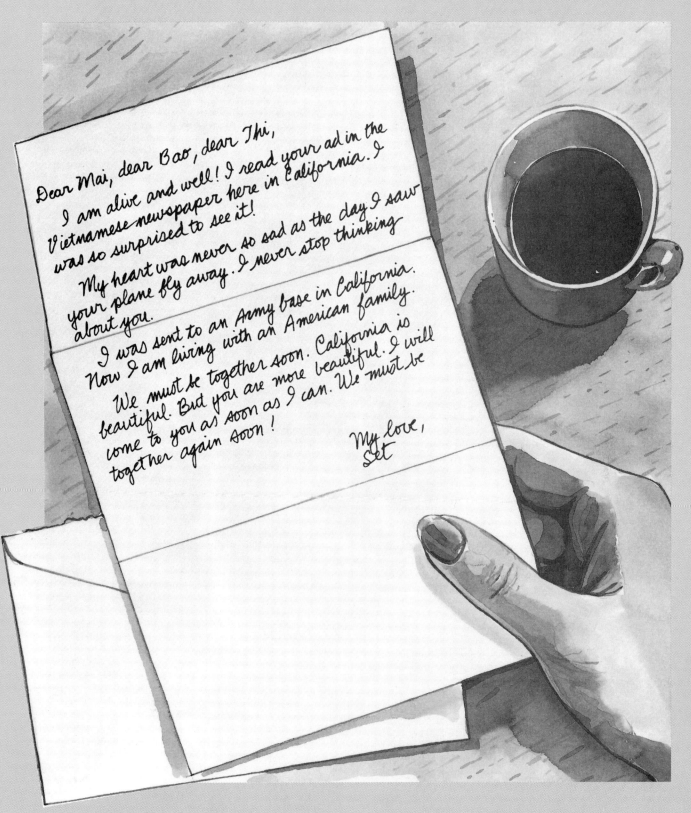

Dear Mai, dear Bao, dear Thi,

I am alive and well! I read your ad in the Vietnamese newspaper here in California. I was so surprised to see it!

My heart was never so sad as the day I saw your plane fly away. I never stop thinking about you.

I was sent to an Army base in California. Now I am living with an American family.

We must be together soon. California is beautiful. But you are more beautiful. I will come to you as soon as I can. We must be together again soon!

My love,
Set

— Part 2 —

Together Again

Mai was so happy. A year ago her world had fallen apart. Seeing Set again would be a dream come true.

Eight days went by. Still no Set. "I hope he is all right," thought Mai.

It was Monday morning. Mai got up for work. She looked out the window. The sun was just coming up. The street was almost empty. But way down the street, a small man was walking slowly. Mai wondered if it could be Set.

She got dressed very quickly. She combed her long, dark hair. Then the doorbell rang. The man walking down the street *had* been Set!

Bao and Thi got to the door first. They were not sure who the man was. They were very small and had not seen their father for a year. Set picked up both of them.

"Daddy!" It was the first time little Thi had ever said that word. Set was so happy, he couldn't speak. Then he saw Mai.

Theme 5

Mai stood at the top of the steps. She watched the children and Set together again.

Then she walked down, one step at a time. Set just stood there. He smiled. Then he let the children down and ran to meet his wife.

They didn't say a word. They held each other close. They didn't want to let go ever again. They held each other to make up for every day of the year gone by.

Then little Thi said, "I'm hungry!"

The whole family went into the apartment. Mai called the chicken farm. She stayed home from work that day. The family ate a big breakfast together. They had so much to talk about. There was nothing but hope in everyone's heart.

What do you think the family talked about at breakfast? With a partner, write a short conversation. All the family members should say something. Read your conversation to a small group. The group can act it out.

Pronouns take the place of people or things in sentences. Here are some common pronouns.

I	we/us	our/ours	myself
he/she/it	you	yours	yourself
her/him	they/them	his/hers	himself/herself

As you read the following story, watch for the pronouns.

A Woman of Valor

When my great-great-grandmother, Elizabeth Morgan, turned 100 years old, we had a celebration in our family. She was born in 1895 in Montgomery, Alabama. More than 200 people gathered in Montgomery to help us celebrate. I was glad that I was there. My name is George Robinson, and I am thirteen years old. As I listened to my great-great-grandmother speak, it was like living through the whole twentieth century. Here are some of the things she said on her one hundredth birthday.

"I remember so many wonderful people and places. During World War I, my father encouraged me to go to France to work as an ambulance driver. I met my husband in France. He was wounded, and I drove him to the hospital.

"I will never forget my mother. She always told me that I could be as smart as the boys in my class. My mother was proud of me when I stood up with lots of other women for a woman's right to vote. We stood in front of the White House. That was in 1919, and we weren't afraid to look right at President Wilson and say to him, 'Equal rights for women!'

Art Math Music
Science Social Studies
LANGUAGE ARTS

Theme 5

"I was there in 1963 when Dr. Martin Luther King, Jr. gave his 'I Have a Dream' speech in Washington, D.C. What a great day that was. Black and white Americans stood together—more than two hundred thousand of us. We said we wanted to live peacefully together.

"But peace didn't come. President Kennedy was killed in November of 1963, then Dr. King was killed in 1968. In some ways, it's hard to live to be 100. You see too many bad things. They frighten you.

"But I don't let myself think that way too long. I say to myself, Elizabeth, you have seen a man walk on the moon. You have seen a black man run for president of the United States. You have seen your children and grandchildren go to college and become successful.

"I don't wish for another hundred years. Computers, VCRs, and bank machines are all so complicated to me. I can't keep up with them. But I hope I'm around for many more years to share the love and happiness I feel being here with all of you."

When Grandma stopped talking, everyone clapped for her. Many people were crying. She is a special woman, and I'm very glad I know her.

Read the questions and write the answers on a separate piece of paper.

1. How old is Elizabeth Morgan?
2. What does she remember?
3. How does she feel about her long life?
4. How does her great-great-grandson feel about her?

Asia, the Largest Continent

Asia is the largest continent on the earth. It is also the most populous. More than 3 billion (3,000,000,000) people live in Asia. The people of Asia speak many different languages and have many different cultures and customs.

Asia is divided into six different regions: Southwest Asia, South Asia, East Asia, Southeast Asia, North Asia, and Central Asia. In this theme, you read a story about a family from Vietnam. Vietnam is in Southeast Asia.

Use the color-coded key and the map to name the regions where other Asian countries are located.

Languages of Asia	
Mandarin	spoken by 884 million people
Hindi	spoken by more than 330 million people
Arabic	spoken by more than 190 million people
Bengali	spoken by more than 100 million people
Malay-Indonesian	spoken by more than 100 million people
Japanese	spoken by more than 100 million people

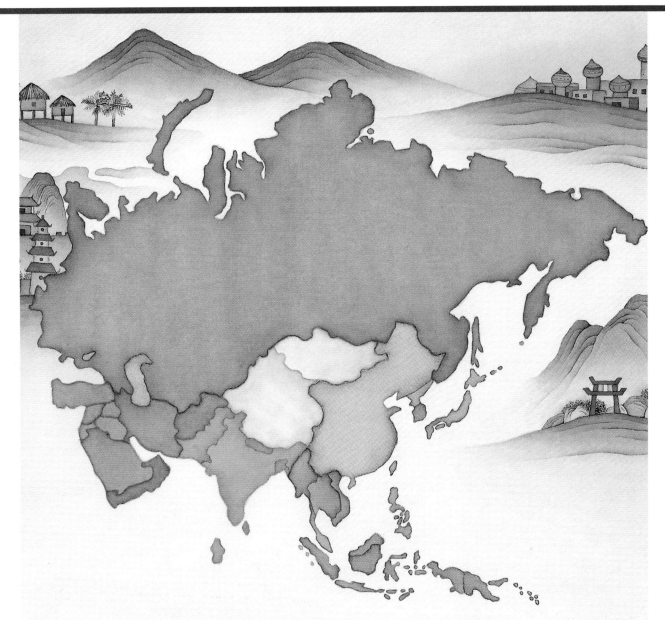

Use the map. Work with a partner to answer these questions.

1. In what region of Asia is China?
2. In what region of Asia is Japan?
3. In what region of Asia is India?
4. In what region of Asia is Thailand?
5. In what region of Asia is Saudi Arabia?

Answer True or False.

6. Siberia is in Southwest Asia.
7. Malaysia is in Central Asia.
8. South Korea is in East Asia.
9. Israel is in Southwest Asia.
10. Pakistan is in East Asia.

MAP KEY

Southwest Asia

South Asia

East Asia

Southeast Asia

North Asia

Central Asia

FLIGHT SONG

LOIS LENSKI

Sing of the mountains, so lovely to see,
Sing of the river, the grass and the tree;
Sing of the forest, the hill and the plain,
Sing of the beauty of ripening grain.

Sing of the clouds, the blue sky and the sun,
Sing of the cars and the trains as they run;
Sing of the cities with buildings so tall,
Sing of the country, of homes large and small.

Art Math Music
Science Social Studies
LANGUAGE ARTS

Sing of the people of many a race,
Sing of the sorrow and joy on each face;
Sing of their courage, their strength and their pain,
Sing of their children, their hope and their gain.

Sing of America, the land of the free,
Sing of her beauty and greatness-to-be;
Sing of America, the land of the free,
Sing of her beauty and greatness-to-be.

YOUR TURN What would you like to sing about? What makes you feel happy or
proud about where you live? Talk about it with a small group.

ALL STAR NEWS

Teen Speak

WE ASKED OLDER TEENS: WHAT WAS A DUMB THING YOU DID TO BE "COOL"?

"I went out for wrestling last year. I shaved my head so the older guys would think I was cool. Well, they didn't call me cool. They called me 'fool'! I felt really foolish, too. Now I know that I should just be myself."

Thuy L., age 14,
Orlando, Florida

"When I was 12, I wasn't fat, but I was gaining weight. I went on a diet. All I talked about was my weight. I was no fun to hang out with. Finally, a counselor helped me understand that I was just growing up—fast. I joined the gymnastics team to stay in shape."

Josie C., age 13,
Austin, Texas

"Last year, some of my friends started to smoke. I finally tried a cigarette. Boy, was I sorry! It tasted terrible, and I threw up! My mother almost killed me when I got home. She could smell the smoke on me. I won't try that again. You don't have to smoke to be cool."

Velma C., age 15,
Memphis, Tennessee

Just Joking

What has a thousand legs, but can't walk?

Five hundred pairs of pants!

Poetry Corner

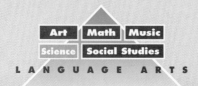

Nicely, nicely, nicely, away in the east, the rain clouds care for the little corn plants as a mother cares for her baby.

Zuni Corn Ceremony

Art Math Music
Science Social Studies

LANGUAGE ARTS

News From All Over

Families from many countries come to live in the USA.

AMAZING FACTS!

- 32 million people in the U.S. (13%) speak languages other than English at home.

- Since 1901, 30% of the U.S. Nobel Prize winners have been immigrants.

- More than 100 languages are spoken in the school systems of New York City, Chicago, Los Angeles, and Fairfax, VA.

TOP TEN COUNTRIES FOR IMMIGRANTS IN THE 1990s:

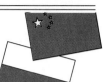

Mexico	22.0%
Vietnam	8.0%
Philippines	6.3%
Dominican Republic	4.3%
China	4.0%
India	3.8%
El Salvador	2.7%
Poland	2.6%
United Kingdom	2.1%

CITIES WHERE MORE THAN HALF THE POPULATION IS FOREIGN-BORN:

Miami, FL	60%
Huntington Park, CA	59%
Union City, NJ	55%
Monterey Park, CA	52%
Miami Beach, FL	51%
Santa Ana, CA	51%

QUILLING

Quilling is the craft of making colorful beads out of paper. Try using magazines and wrapping paper. Just cut strips, glue them, and roll them up. Then string them into beautiful necklaces, bracelets, or earrings!

You will need:

- pencil and ruler
- shiny magazines or sheets of heavy wrapping paper
- scissors
- glue
- Q-Tips
- waxed paper
- juice-box straws
- string long enough for a necklace

1. Draw tall, skinny triangles about $1\frac{1}{4}$ inches wide and 11 inches high. Draw them on the side of the paper that you don't want to show.

2. Cut out each triangle. You will need at least 22 triangles to make a necklace that will fit over your head.

3. Lay a triangle down on waxed paper with the side that you want to show facing up. Cover the triangle with a light coating of glue.

4. Turn over the paper triangle. Begin rolling the wide end around a straw until the whole triangle is rolled up. Slide the straw out.

5. Make more triangle beads this way. Let the beads dry.

6. Thread your beads onto the string to make a necklace. Tie the ends. Put on your colorful necklace and show it to your friends!

Dear All Star News:

My friends like rap music. They think it's cool. I don't. Should I pretend I like it? What will my friends say?

Country Joe

THEMEWORK TEAMWORK

1. **Make a photo essay on a new place.** Work with a partner. Make a photo essay on a new place. Choose a place you've never seen before. What are the people like? What do they do every day? What do they eat? What days do they celebrate? Find pictures to go with your words. Share your essay with a small group.

MONTANA

2. **Make a collage.** Draw pictures or cut pictures out of magazines of the people and things you like about the United States. Write a sentence or two about each one. Share your collage with a small group.

3. **Use the Process Writing Portfolio.** Look in your portfolio for a list of ideas and writing topics related to this theme.

4. **Research and report.** Find out more about Asian languages and cultures. Choose one country to explore. Write a report or make an oral presentation to the class. Work with a partner or by yourself.

A Bad Day for Abdul

▶ LISTEN

Listen to the beginning of the story. Tell whether each sentence is **True** or **False**.

1. The students all smiled at Abdul.
2. Abdul understood what the teacher said to him.
3. Abdul opened his science book.
4. The teacher wanted Abdul to read his book.
5. The students laughed at Abdul.
6. Abdul had three more classes to go.

▶ SPEAK

Tell about Abdul's first class. What class was it? Why did he hate the class?

LANGUAGE ARTS

READ

At last, the day was over. Abdul hurried home. His mother said, "You look upset, Abdul. What happened at school?"

Abdul answered, "Mom, I hate school. I don't understand what anyone says to me. The other kids laugh at me. I don't want to go back." His mother said, "I know. It's going to be okay. Your teacher called your uncle this afternoon and told him about some new classes at school to help students learn English. She said the classes would help you understand and be able to talk to the other students."

A smile came to Abdul's face, "You mean they will help me learn English?" "Yes," his mother replied. "They'll teach you English and help you with your other classes, too."

"When can I go to these classes?" asked Abdul.

"Next week," said his mother. "You will go to them part of every day at school. Mrs. Nunez will show you where to go. You can ask her for help when you need it."

Abdul smiled. Suddenly his bad day was looking better.

WRITE

Write about your first day in a new school. What happened? How did you feel?

THINK

Why didn't Abdul want to go back to school?

New Faces, New Places

FEELINGS AND EMOTIONS
WORDS AND MUSIC BY BOB SCHNEIDER

Chorus
Feelings, emotions,
Got so many feelings, like waves upon the ocean.
Feelings, emotions,
Got so many feelings, like waves upon the ocean.

It makes me happy when I'm singing with my friends,
Talk about feelings, talk about emotions.
Oh, so happy, want to do it again and again,
Talk about feelings, talk about emotions.
It makes me angry when my mama picks on me,
Talk about feelings, talk about emotions.
Oh, so angry, I want to climb a tree,
Talk about feelings, talk about emotions.

Chorus

It makes me sad when my friends all go away,
Talk about feelings, talk about emotions.
Oh, so sad, I wish that they could stay,
Talk about feelings, talk about emotions.
It makes me shy when I'm in a new place,
Talk about feelings, talk about emotions.
Oh, so shy, I want to hide my face,
Talk about feelings, talk about emotions.

Chorus

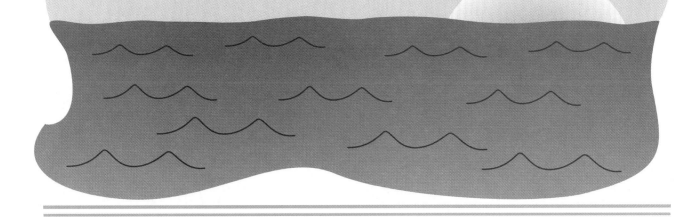

Theme 5

Reading Corner

Try these terrific books!

The Lampfish of Twill
by Janet T. Lisle
An environmental fantasy you won't forget.

Life In the Rainforests
by Lucy Baker
Animals, plants, and people in a unique habitat.

As Dead As A Dodo
by Paul Rice and Peter Mayle
Extinct animals—and how they got that way!

Animals in Danger

ADAPTED FROM THE ARTICLE "ENDANGERED SPECIES"
IN **KIDS DISCOVER** JUNE/JULY 1995

Imagine this. The year is 2050. You are reading to your granddaughter. On the cover of the book is an elephant. Your granddaughter looks at you. She asks, "What's that?"

"That's an elephant," you say sadly. "But there are no elephants left. They are extinct. They are gone forever."

Can this really happen in the future? The answer is yes.

Many animals like the elephants are in danger.

More and more people are crowding the earth.

The air and water are becoming dirty.

This dirt is called pollution.

Pollution is killing the animals.

The land where animals live is disappearing

People are taking wild animals from where they live.

They want them for pets.

People are killing them for food or for sport.

Sometimes the animals are killed only for their skins, fur,

feathers, or horns.

Many animals are in danger of dying out—forever.

Some people say that more than one million kinds of animals

will become extinct in just the next five years.

Here are a few that are in danger.

Art Math Music
Science Social Studies

LANGUAGE ARTS

IN THE AMERICAS

The Quetzal of Central America

This bird has no place to live. People have cut down the trees that were its home. It is often sold to people who collect birds. Sometimes it is killed just for its beautiful feathers.

The Macaw in Brazil

The macaw is disappearing because it can't find nuts to eat. These nuts grow on a tree that is also disappearing. The farmers are cutting down the tree. Macaws are also caught and sold. One macaw brings $10,000.

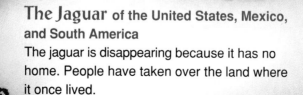

The Jaguar of the United States, Mexico, and South America

The jaguar is disappearing because it has no home. People have taken over the land where it once lived.

In Africa

The Chimpanzee

The chimpanzee is dying out because the land where it lives is disappearing. It is also being hunted for sport. Chimps are sold to zoos and to people who want them for pets.

The Elephant

The elephant is killed for its white tusks made of ivory. Ivory is used to make jewelry and other things.

IN ASIA

The Giant Panda in Southern China

The land where the panda lives is disappearing. People are taking the pandas' land for farming. They cut down the bamboo trees that the pandas eat. Now it is hard for the pandas to find food and shelter.

The Gray Wolf

Farmers kill gray wolves because they eat livestock. In some places, gray wolves hunt large, hoofed animals like deer and bison.

In the Wild

A

A WEATHER MAP

What will the weather be like tomorrow?

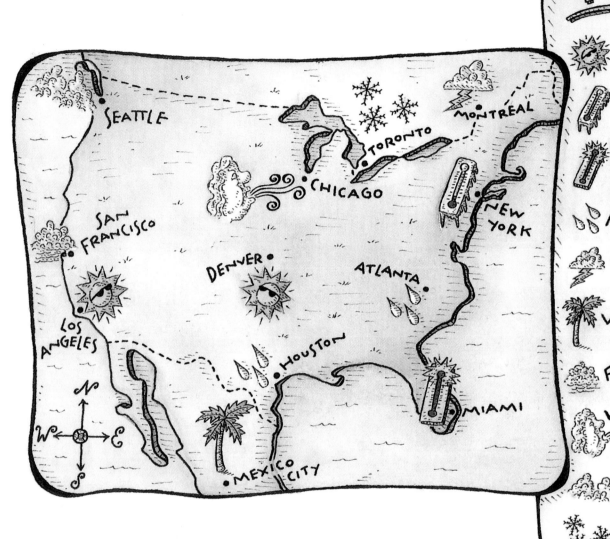

KEY

SUNNY
COLD
HOT
RAINING
STORMY
WARM
FOGGY
WINDY
CLOUDY
SNOWY

Look at the weather map. Tell what the weather will be.

What will the weather be like in each of these cities tomorrow?

1. San Francisco WINDY Cloudy
2. Toronto winter SNOwy
3. Los Angeles Sunny
4. Miami Hot
5. Seattle Cloudy

6. Houston RAining
7. Mexico City Warm
8. New York cold
9. Montreal lighting Stormy
10. Chicago windy

Art Math Music
Science Social Studies

LANGUAGE ARTS

Theme **6**

WILD WEATHER

Sometimes the weather is warm and friendly. Sometimes the weather is wild and dangerous.

A flood is the result of too much rain. When it rains for many days, rivers and lakes overflow. Flood waters cause a lot of damage to houses, buildings, roads, and crops.

A drought is the opposite problem from a flood. A drought is the result of little or no rain. If it doesn't rain, plants and animals will die. A drought is a dangerous condition for farmers and ranchers.

A hurricane is an extremely dangerous storm with high winds and torrential rain. Hurricanes form over the ocean. They roar up the east coast of the U.S. from the Caribbean. Many hurricanes remain at sea, but hurricanes often travel inland. When a hurricane hits land, it can destroy everything for miles around.

A tornado is another kind of wind storm. States in the middle of the U.S. experience many tornadoes. Tornadoes are very dangerous. They can destroy anything in their path. Tornadoes make a loud, roaring sound like a speeding train.

A big winter snowstorm is called a blizzard. A blizzard has a lot of snow and high wind. The wind blows the snow into huge snowdrifts. Airports close; roads close. People can lose electricity, heat, and phones. A snowfall can be pretty, but a blizzard is a winter storm you don't want to be caught in!

Tornado in the midwest

The Amazing Rain Forest

A tropical rain forest is an amazing place. Most rain forests are in South America, Africa, and Asia. More than half of the plants and animals in the world live in rain forests. The trees grow straight up to 100 feet or more. At the top, the leaves and branches make a tent that shades the forest floor.

These forests are called rain forests because they actually help create rain.

1. The rain falls on the leaves at the top.
2. The water drips down to the forest floor.
3. Some of this water drains into the streams and rivers. Some water goes into the soil and back up the tree trunk through the roots.
4. Lots of moisture stays at the top in the leaves. This moisture evaporates and forms clouds.
5. The water in the clouds falls again as rain.

Do you remember how much rain falls each year in the Puerto Rican rain forest?

Art | Math | Music
Science | Social Studies
LANGUAGE ARTS

People are destroying an area of rain forest as big as Pennsylvania every year. All the rain forests in the world may be gone in 50 years! People cut down rain forest trees to build furniture and houses. People cut down the trees to clear land for cattle. Then they sell the beef to other countries.

It takes several hundred years for trees to grow back as big as they were. When the trees are gone, the soil washes away. Plants and animals die. Carbon dioxide in the air increases because there aren't enough trees to absorb it. Too much carbon dioxide traps the sun's heat on the earth. This global warming makes temperatures rise. Floods and droughts are the result.

Rain forests are important to the health of the whole planet. You can help protect the rain forest. Write to:

Tree Amigos Project
143 Bostwick, NE
Grand Rapids, MI 49503

Find out how you can "adopt" acres of rain forest.

Animal Rescue Success Stories

ADAPTED FROM THE ARTICLE "ENDANGERED SPECIES"
IN **KIDS DISCOVER** JUNE/JULY 1995

Not all animals in danger become extinct.
Here are some success stories.

The Manatee

Many manatee were killed by speeding
motorboats. There is now a safe place near
Florida where the manatee can live. The
manatee is playful and likes to be petted.

The Koala

The koala lives in trees in
Australia. When people cut down
the trees, the koalas lost their
homes. Hunters also killed them
for their fur. Now there are many
laws to protect the koala.

The Loggerhead Turtle

Loggerhead turtles lay their eggs on beaches. When
too many people are on the beaches, the turtles can't
lay their eggs and no new turtles are born. To help save
them, some beaches are now only for the turtles and
other animals. People have to swim and sunbathe
somewhere else.

Art | Math | Music
Science | Social Studies

L A N G U A G E   A R T S

Bluebirds

Bluebirds were hard to find in North America, but now more and more are seen every year. People have put up bird houses where the birds can live and build their nests.

The Humpback Whale

Laws against killing the humpback whale have saved it. Now boats take people out on the ocean to watch the whales swim and play.

How You Can Help

Put up bird houses. You can feed the birds and give them protection.

Cut up plastic rings that hold cans together. Many birds get caught in them.

Plant a tree. Trees put oxygen in the air. Animals and people need oxygen to breathe. Trees are homes for many animals.

Walk, ride a bike, or take a bus. Cars give off a lot of pollution. Pollution in the air falls back to earth as acid rain. This rain poisons the land and water.

Recycle. Soda cans can be used again. Newspapers can be ground up and made into newsprint. Plastic bottles can be made into insulation for sleeping bags.

 **YOUR TURN** Write to these groups for more information about what you can do to help animals and the Earth.

National Wildlife Federation
1400 16th Street, NW
Washington, DC 20036-2266

Sierra Club
730 Polk Street
San Francisco, CA 94109

The Acid Rain Foundation, Inc.
1410 Varsity Drive
Raleigh, NC 27606

Renew America
1400 16th Street, NW, Suite 700
Washington, DC 20036

In My Mountains

In my mountains,
Where the wind blows cold and fresh,
The scent of wild flowers floats on the breeze,
Animals are roaming everywhere,
Fish are swimming in the streams,
Streams that are pure and clear,
Streams that are cold.

The sound of night
With stars shining bright,
Of the stream gurgling on its way,
The animals creeping in the distance,
And the smell of the dying campfire,
Yes, I love my mountains.

Jill Yokomizo
Cleveland School
Oakland, CA

ALL STAR NEWS

Teen Speak

WE ASKED KIDS: WHAT'S THE MOST SERIOUS PROBLEM IN OUR ENVIRONMENT?

"It's the air. We are polluting the air we need to breathe to stay alive."
Kathy S., age 14,
Portland, Oregon

"Garbage. We are running out of room to put our trash. Many landfills in the U.S. are almost full."
Betty L., age 13,
San Francisco, California

"The rain forests are disappearing. This affects the whole Earth."
Glen D., age 13,
Colorado Springs, Colorado

"Animals are dying. I love chimps, and I can't stand the thought that they might all disappear."
José G., age 12,
Sarasota, Florida

Just Joking

Five big men were standing under an umbrella. How come none of them got wet?

It wasn't raining.

We asked 100 kids: Where would you most like to spend an outdoor vacation?

Disney World	47%
Alaska	14%
Yosemite National Park	13%
Colorado River	10%
Hawaii	10%
Florida Keys	8%

Art | Math | Music
Science | Social Studies

LANGUAGE ARTS

News From All Over

Native Americans Protect Wild Rice

AMAZING FACTS!

- The Komodo dragon is the world's largest lizard. It can stretch out the length of a compact car!

- A snow leopard can jump 50 feet. The record for a human jump is 29 feet, 2 1/2 inches.

- After a good drink of your blood, a mosquito's weight can increase up to four times.

- A future Hawaiian island is forming about a half mile under the ocean. It will take around 30,000 years for it to rise to the surface.

The Chippewa people live on the White Earth Reservation in Minnesota.

They are hand-harvesting wild rice like their ancestors did. Hand-harvesting protects the water. It preserves surrounding plant life. it uses no pesticides or chemical fertilizers.

The Chippewa float through the rice beds in canoes. They use 28-inch long ricing sticks to knock the ripe rice off the stalks. "I have harvested rice for 35 years," says Margaret Smith. "It's hard work."

Margaret Smith and Winona LaDuke started to sell the hand-harvested rice in 1985. The response was terrific. People told them that the pure, natural rice was just what they wanted.

"Instead of trying to tame the wild, we're showing people how to respect it," says LaDuke. "This helps both the Chippewa and the environment."

EARTH DAY

Earth Day is April 22, but you can help the planet every day of the year. Write to these addresses for more information.

U.S. ENVIRONMENTAL PROTECTION AGENCY
Office of Education
201 M Street, SW A108
Washington, DC 20460

TREE AMIGOS PROJECT
143 Bostwick, NE
Grand Rapids, MI 49503

KEEP AMERICA BEAUTIFUL
9 West Broad Street
Stamford, CT 06892

KIDS FOR SAVING THE EARTH
P. O. Box 47247
Plymouth, MN 55447

TRACK YOUR TRASH

For one week, keep track of everything you throw away. Make lists of items in at least four categories: food, plastic, glass, and paper. What kind of waste do you throw away most? Does most of your waste come from one source, say, wrappings and other packages? Can you think of ways to cut back on what you throw away? What parts of your trash could you recycle?

118

Dear All Star News,

My friends sometimes steal little things. The things aren't expensive. They could pay for them, but they don't. They say, "It's no big deal." What do you think?

Worried in Dallas

THEMEWORK TEAMWORK

1. **Choose a project.** With a small group, do a "save the animals and birds" project. First choose a project. Then bring to school the things you need. Here are some ideas. Think of your own ideas, too.

   A. **Make a birdhouse. Hang it outside a window of your classroom.**

   B. **Grow flowers in a box for insects and birds. Put it outside a window of your classroom.**

   C. **Plant a tree on the school grounds. Make sure your principal says it's OK.**

   D. **Sell cookies to raise money for your local zoo or animal shelter.**

2. **Research and report.** Choose an animal from the articles in this theme. Find out all you can about the animal. Write a short report. Illustrate your report with photos or drawings. Share your report with the class.

3. **Write a letter.** Write a letter to one of the organizations on page 118. Ask what you can do to help animals or the earth. Share the information you receive with your family. Talk to them about what you can all do to help animals or the earth.

4. **Use the Process Writing Portfolio.** Look in your portfolio for a list of ideas and writing topics related to this theme.

Wildlife Savers

• • • • • • • • • • •

Kids in Walnut Creek, California, work in a special museum
for wild animals that need help.

 LISTEN

Listen to the beginning of the story. Tell whether each
sentence is **True** or **False**.

1. The special museum in Walnut Creek, California, is for
   wild animals that need help.
2. Most of the animals stay at the museum all their
   lives.
3. The animals' real home is the wild.
4. Only adults can be workers at the museum.
5. Teenagers are not allowed to feed the animals.
6. One of Emily Rainero's favorite animals is the parrot.

 SPEAK

Tell about the museum for wild animals in Walnut Creek,
California. What is special about it? What do people
do there?

READ

Some kids work in the Pet Library. That's where people can borrow animals during their visit.

Worker Nic Fleming likes to show the king snake to visitors. "The king snake is my favorite animal," he said. He likes to wrap a king snake around himself. Children come right up to him and touch the snake. Adults usually stand back. Nic thinks this is really funny.

Allyson Hogue loves the animals, too, but she doesn't like to clean their cages. She said, "It's the grossest part of the job." But she really likes working at the museum. The barn owl is one of her favorite animals. Allyson also likes showing the visitors how they can live peacefully with nature.

WRITE

What animal in the wild is your favorite? Write about it. What does it look like? What does it like to eat? Where does it live?

THINK

Why do you think the children come up to the king snake but the adults stand back?

The animals go back to their real home in the wild when they can take care of themselves. Why is this important?

LISTEN TO THE WATER

WORDS AND MUSIC BY BOB SCHNEIDER

Chorus
Listen to the water;
Listen to the water;
Rolling down the river.
Listen to the water;
Listen to the water;
Rolling down the river.

We saw some birds by the waterside;
We saw some birds by the waterside;
We saw some birds by the waterside;
Oh, oh by the waterside,
Oh, oh by the waterside.

Chorus

We saw some fish by the waterside;
We saw some fish by the waterside;
We saw some fish by the waterside;
Oh, oh by the waterside,
Oh, oh by the waterside.

Chorus

We saw some ducks by the waterside;
We saw some ducks by the waterside;
We saw some ducks by the waterside;
Oh, oh by the waterside,
Oh, oh by the waterside.

Chorus

Art Math Music
Science Social Studies

LANGUAGE ARTS

GRAMMAR SUMMARY

THEME 1 LOOK AT ME

Letters Review

Aa Bb Cc Dd Ee Ff Gg Hh Ii Jj Kk Ll Mm Nn Oo Pp Qq Rr Ss Tt Uu Vv Ww Xx Yy Zz

Number Review, pages 8-9, 17

Cardinal Numbers

1 = one	11 = eleven	21 = twenty-one
2 = two	12 = twelve	30 = thirty
3 = three	13 = thirteen	40 = forty
4 = four	14 = fourteen	50 = fifty
5 = five	15 = fifteen	60 = sixty
6 = six	16 = sixteen	70 = seventy
7 = seven	17 = seventeen	80 = eighty
8 = eight	18 = eighteen	90 = ninety
9 = nine	19 = nineteen	100 = one hundred
10 = ten	20 = twenty	1,000 = one thousand

Ordinal Numbers

1st = first
2nd = second
3rd = third
4th = fourth
5th = fifth
6th = sixth

Simple Present Tense, pages 4-6

Subject	Verb
I You We They	**live** in New York.
He She It	**lives** in New York.

Present Tense of be, pages 4-6, 12-15

Subject	Verb	
I	am	
You	are	a student.
He	is	
She	is	
It	is	an island.
We You They	are	in the United States.

Possessive Adjectives, pages 4-6, 8-9

Subject Pronoun	Possessive Adjectives
I	my
you	your
he	his
she	her
it	its
we	our
you	your
they	their

THEME 2 YOUR FAMILY, MY FAMILY

Prepositions of Place, pages 28-29
Prepositions of place tell where something is. These are common prepositions of place.

in	on	under
beside	between	

The ring is **in** the box.
The ball is **between** a chair and a table.

Present Progressive, pages 32-33
Use the present progressive to talk about an action that is happening now (as you are speaking).

Subject	*be*	Base Form of Verb + *-ing*
I	am	
You	are	
He She It	is	eating.
We You They	are	

124

Regular Present Verbs: *-s* and *-es*, pages 48-49

Add *-s* to form the third person singular of most verbs.

> She play**s** soccer.

Add *-es* to words that end in *ch, s, sh, x,* or *z.*

> She teach**es** at a daycare center.

Here are some regular present verbs.

eat	eats	teach	teaches
play	plays	go	goes
walk	walks	watch	watches
ride	rides	practice	practices
pick	picks	wash	washes
clean	cleans	write	writes
help	helps	wake	wakes

Days of the Week Review, pages 48-49

Sunday
Monday
Tuesday
Wednesday
Thursday
Friday
Saturday

Compound Words, pages 44-46

A word or word group with two or more parts that act as a unit.

Here are some compound words from Themes 1, 2, and 3.

baseball	tryouts	workshop	weekend
rain forest	sunlight	basketball	lighthouse
dog house	fireplace	drugstore	hairdresser

THEME 4 HOPES AND DREAMS

Regular Past Tense, pages 68-69

Use the simple past tense to talk about an event that happened in the past.

Subject	Base Form of Verb + *-ed, -d, -ied*
I You He She It We You They	cook**ed.** arriv**ed.** cr**ied.**

There are three ways to pronounce past endings: /-t/, /-d/, and /-id/
Here are some examples:

/t/	/d/	/id/
laughed	played	wanted
missed	skied	attended
wished	snowed	rested

Irregular Past Tense, pages 64-67
Here are some irregular past verbs.

come	came	ride	rode
get	got	sing	sang
go	went	speak	spoke
grow	grew	wake	woke
hold	held	write	wrote
kneel	knelt		

THEME 5 NEW FACES, NEW PLACES

Modals, pages 84-85
Modals are words that come before verbs. They can change the meanings of the verbs in some way. For example, modals can express ability or possibility. Here are some examples.

He **can** swim but he **can't** dive.
Ten years ago she **couldn't** use a computer. Now she **can.**

Pronouns, pages 90-91
Pronouns take the place of people or things in a sentence. Here are some common pronouns.

I	we/us	our/ours	myself
her/him	you	yours	yourself
he/she/it	they/them	his/hers	himself/herself

THEME 6, IN THE WILD

Future Tense: *be/going to*, pages 108-109

Subject	Be	Going to	
I	am		
You	are		
He	is		
She	is	going to	school tomorrow.
You	are		
We	are		
They	are		
It	is		rain tomorrow.

INDEX

(continued)

WRITING

Creating a collage 99
Creating a photo essay 19, 39, 59, 79, 99
Creating a poster 19
Creative writing 79, 89
Descriptive/narrative writing 81, 101, 121
Process writing 19, 39, 59, 79, 99, 119
Research and reports 39, 99, 119
Writing a letter 38, 41, 78, 111, 114, 118, 119
Writing about a theme 19, 39, 59, 79, 99, 119
Writing about yourself 19, 21, 38

LEARNING IN THE CONTENT AREAS

LEARNING STRATEGIES/STUDY SKILLS

Activating prior knowledge (throughout)
Collaborating with classmates 19, 39, 59, 79, 99, 119
Creating graphic organizers 19, 37, 39, 59, 79, 99, 116, 119
Doing research 92-93, 108
Interpreting charts/graphics 8-9, 36, 37, 92-93
Interpreting maps 4-5, 12, 92-93, 108
Recording observations 10-11
Sharing information with classmates 6, 7, 15, 19, 27, 33, 55, 67, 74
Summarizing 20, 40, 60, 80, 100, 120
Taking a survey 19, 37, 39, 59, 79
Taking notes 15

LITERATURE

Amazing Facts 17, 37, 57, 77, 97, 117
Autobiography 4-6
Biography 80-81
Fantasy 64-67
Fiction 84-89
Jokes 16, 36, 56, 76, 96, 116
News articles 17, 37, 57, 77, 97, 127
Nonfiction essays 12-15, 72-74, 104-107, 112-114
Photo essays 4-6, 12-15, 52-55, 72-74, 104-107
Poetry 7, 16, 34, 35, 47, 76, 94-95, 96, 115
Prose poem 24-27, 64-67
Songs 22, 42, 62, 82, 102, 122
Speech 75

MATH

Interpreting graphs/charts 8-9, 36, 37, 92-93, 116
Percentages 36, 97, 116
Statistics 17, 37, 77, 92, 97, 117
Measurement 17, 31

SCIENCE

Learning about

endangered animals 104-107, 112-113
food pyramid 30-31
photography 78
rain forest 110-111
recycling/pollution 114, 116-119
vitamins/healthy eating 30-31

Projects

creating a mini-rain forest 10-11
finding the "sweet spot" (vibrations) 50-51
making a healthy recipe (salsa) 31

SOCIAL STUDIES

Learning about

Africa 64-67
Asia 92-93
Chinese birthday celebration 34
climate 12-15, 110-111
geography 4-6, 12-15, 17, 92-93, 104-107, 108, 110-111
immigrant experiences 17, 84-89, 94-95, 97
Martin Luther King, Jr. 75, 80-81
Native American culture 18, 24-27, 57, 70-71, 117
photography 78
Puerto Rico 12-15
U.S. History 80-81, 90-91
UNICEF 78

Projects

creating a Chippewa dream catcher 70-71
creating a Native American owner stick 18

LINGUISTIC SKILLS

Adjectives 109
Future with *will* 108
Possessives 8-9
Prepositions: *in, on, under, beside, between* 28-29
Pronouns: *subject, object, reflexive* 90-91
Question word *what* 8-9
Questions with *did* 68-69
Simple past: *regular* and *irregular* 68-69
Simple present: with *-s, -es* 48-49
Verb "to be" 4-6, 12-15

HOLISTIC ASSESSMENT

Listening/speaking/reading/writing/thinking 20-21, 40-41, 60-61, 80-81, 100-101, 120-121